Chihuahua

By Ann Hearn

W9-BSE-119

BREEDERS' BEST
A KENNEL CLUB BOOK™

CHIHUAHUA

ISBN: 1-59378-914-9

Copyright © 2004
Kennel Club Books, LLC
308 Main Street, Allenhurst, NJ 07711 USA
Printed in South Korea

PHOTOS BY:
Isabelle Français,
Carol Ann Johnson,
and Bernd Brinkmann.

DRAWINGS BY:
Yolyanko el Habanero

Contents

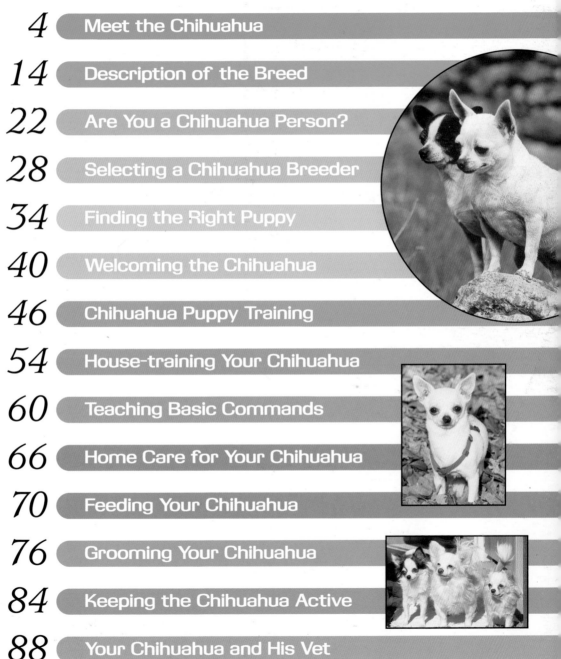

Meet the Chihuahua

There are numerous theories about the origin of the Chihuahua, but, as its name suggests, as a distinct breed it undoubtedly stems from Chihuahua, a Mexican state abutting western Texas and New Mexico. Many different possibilities regarding the distant history of the breed have been thrown into the melting pot. Some believe it was taken to Mexico by the Chinese, so that, in effect, it has Chinese origins. Others consider

Whether or not the Chihuahua is actually related to the fennec fox, the two do bear some resemblance to each other, especially in the ears and eyes.

it to have a link with Peruvian and Mexican hairless dogs. Although none of these is as small as the diminutive Chihuahua, occasionally smaller dogs appear in the smallest of the three size varieties of the Mexican Hairless (Xoloitzcuintli).

Several theories exist about the Chihuahua's development, but the breed is most closely connected with originating in Mexico.

Another theory that could be plausible is that the breed's ancestors came from Egypt or the Sudan, and that they were taken through the Mediterranean countries to Malta, where a Maltese "pocket dog" was known. Interestingly, the Maltese "pocket dog" and the Chihuahua both have a molera, or a soft spot, in the skull. This molera is the result of the cranial gap not closing as it does in other dogs. Of course, we cannot dismiss the possibility that the Chihuahua may have been taken to Malta, rather than arriving here from Malta.

The longhaired variety was developed after the Chihuahua was first established as a smooth-coated breed.

Perhaps the strangest theory of all is that the breed is actually descended from the fennec fox, a native of Africa's Sahara Desert. The mind boggles. However, before you dismiss this last suggestion as implausible, consider that in the 1980s a fennec fox was successfully bred with a Chihuahua!

There is no doubt that in North America small dogs were highly thought of. This is borne out by the fact that 21 small dogs were found in a single excavation in Kentucky. The graves dated back to 3000 BC. There have been many other excavations that have unearthed small canines, even in Yucatan, and these have been highly significant.

Investigating the more recent history of the Chihuahua, we see that the Toltec empire in Mexico reached its zenith in about 900 AD. The Toltec dog appeared in carvings that have survived in the Monas-tery of Huejotzingo. This was built around 1530. It was con-structed from materials taken from pyramids of Choula, built by the Toltecs. It is located on the highway from Mexico City to Puebla. These carvings show a full view of a head and a full profile of a dog that looks remarkably similar to the Chihuahua we know today.

The Toltec civilization was mainly centered around Tula, close to Mexico City, and it is in this area that most of the earliest finds were made. Dogs were found in old ruins near Casas Grandes. These believed to be the ruins of a palace built by Emperor Montezuma I, who reigned in 1440. From the relics found, it seems that the dog called the Techichi was long-haired, rust-colored and also mute, and there is a theory that a small hairless dog was eventually crossed with the Techichi. This was brought from Asia into Alaska and on to Mexico, and would account for the smaller, smooth-coated and vocal Chihuahuas having come about. It is a theory that can by no means be dismissed.

It seems fairly certain that the Toltec Techichi is the direct ancestor of our very own

the spirits of the dead. Dogs were sacrificed and interred with their masters' remains so that the humans' sins could be transferred to the dogs. This ensured safe passage to the spiritual resting place. For a period of time, wealthy Toltecs

The longhaired variety is said to have developed from crosses with the Pomeranian and Papillon; similarities to both breeds are noticeable.

Chihuahua. The Aztecs conquered the Toltecs and they, too, knew the Techichi, which they used for religious sacrifices along with the hairless dogs. Dogs were sacred icons of the upper classes and were used to expiate sins and as guides for

considered the blue-colored dogs sacred, but the poorer classes had no need of such dogs and are believed to have used them for food, despite their small size.

The Aztec Empire was the first American civilization to fall to the Spanish. Possession was taken, and there is virtually no record of the dogs of the region from the early part of the 16th century. It is thought that dogs were used as a source of food by the Spaniards, but some found refuge with peasant families and others escaped into the wild.

Time moved on, and the Chihuahua miraculously

Whether longhaired or smooth-coated, the same intelligent dog is underneath. The Chihuahua's expression imparts the breed's confidence and "big-dog" attitude.

The breed's name derived from the Mexican state of the same name. The first two pairs of the breed to enter the US were from Chihuahua in Mexico.

The Chihuahua is seen in a wide range of colors, patterns and markings in both coat varieties.

survived, so that by the 19th century it could be found throughout Mexico. American tourists took home two pairs from the State of Chihuahua in the 1850s and dubbed them "Chihuahuas." In 1884, there are records of Mexicans selling these dogs to tourists in the border markets, calling them "Mexican," "Texan" or "Arizona" dogs, depending upon where they were sold!

So the breed found itself in the US, and in 1890 the American Kennel Club's (AKC) stud book makes reference to four unregistered Chihuahuas called Anno, Bob, Eyah and Pepity. Then, in 1894, two more Chihuahuas were recorded, Chihuahueria and Nita. Clearly the breed had captured a steady interest, and the breed was officially recognized by the AKC in 1904. It is poignant that the first Chihuahua ever registered by the AKC was called "Midget"! The Chihuahua Club of America was estab

This precious pair enjoys the view from its vantage point at the top of the Toys!

lished in 1923. In Mexico, the ancestral home of the breed, the Chihuahua was not officially registered until 1934.

In Britain, the Chihuahua had been kept as a pet from the 1850s, but the first one registered was in 1907. A breed club was founded in 1949 but, by then, largely due to World War II, there were only eight registered Chihuahuas in Britain. The breed was not officially recognized until 1954, and its increase in popularity was fairly slow. Then, in 1963, the Chihuahua suddenly rocketed to being the breed with the

In addition to the longer coat over the entire body, the longhaired variety possesses more ruff around the neck and feathering around the ears.

third-highest registration figures in the Toy Group. This popularity among the Toy breeds was only surpassed by the Yorkshire Terrier and Pekingese.

SMOOTH AND LONG COATS

Two coat varieties are well known in today's Chihuahuas, but this was not always the case. Although we learn from excavations that the early Techichi may have had long hair, the breed developed as a smooth one. From crossings with other long-coated Toy breeds, notably the Papillon and possibly also the Pomeranian, a long-coated variety arose. In the US, the smooth- and long-coated varieties were separated in 1952 and in Britain they were separately entered for the first time at Crufts in 1965. A year later, the two varieties were separated in Australia. Interestingly, at least in the last century or so there were no long-coated Chihuahuas in Mexico until about 1959. In some countries, long- and smooth-coated Chihuahuas may be interbred, but in others this is not allowed.

MEET THE CHIHUAHUA

Overview

- Despite various theories of ancestry, the Chihuahua is most commonly considered a breed of Mexican origin.
- The Techichi dog of the Mexican Toltec civilization is likely the Chihuahua's direct ancestor. The Toltecs and Aztecs considered some of these small dogs to be sacred.
- The breed crossed the border into the US in the mid-1850s. Today the breed is among the top Toy breeds in many countries worldwide.
- Crosses with other Toys resulted in a longhaired variety. Today, both the smooth- and long-coated Chihuahuas are well established.

Description of the Breed

"**A** pint-sized canine with a macho streak." This is a rather apt description of the Chihuahua, a thoroughly charming breed, alert, spirited and intelligent, with a loving heart. He is quite full of himself and will stand up to any dog however large. You can only suspect that he isn't even aware of his diminutive size—except when it suits him!

Although the Chihuahua is known as a "head breed," I believe that it is the breed's tiny size that first strikes the casual observer. After all, who doesn't know that the Chihuahua is the smallest breed in

A look into the Chihuahua's eyes tells volumes about his intelligence and attitude. The Chihuahua's expression is truly unforgettable.

the world? Breed standards in different countries vary just slightly, with the AKC's stating simply that this is "a well balanced little dog not to exceed 6 pounds." In Britain, although the breed can be up to 6 lbs, a weight of 2–4 lbs is preferred. The breed standard of Europe's Fédération Cynologique Internationale (FCI), adopted by many countries, points out that only weight is taken into consideration, not height. Weight can be between 500 g and 3 kg (1–6 lbs), with a preference for 1–2 kg (2–4 lbs); dogs weighing over 3 kg (6 lbs) are disqualified from competition.

The smallest breed with the biggest personality, Chihuahuas are natural performers and make popular show dogs. This dog is being trained to the proper show pose or "stack."

Experts consider that the head of the Chihuahua is its most distinguishing feature. Its skull is "apple-domed," its cheeks and jaws lean and its muzzle is fairly short and pointed. There may or may not be a molera, the cranial gap in the skull that has not closed with maturity. The large round eyes do not protrude, and

A typical smooth Chihuahua with correct head, proportions and sickle-like tail carriage.

CHAPTER 2

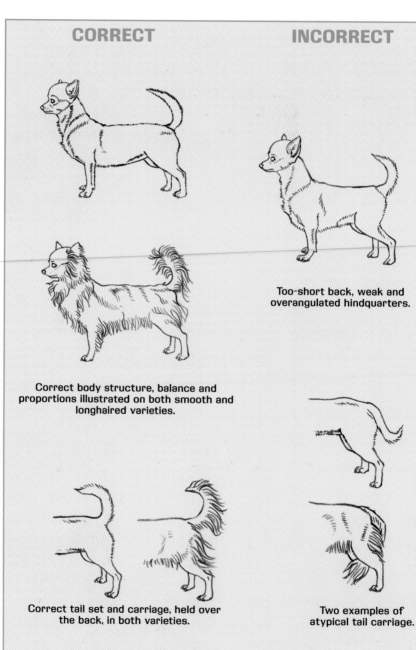

CORRECT

INCORRECT

Correct body structure, balance and proportions illustrated on both smooth and longhaired varieties.

Too-short back, weak and overangulated hindquarters.

Correct tail set and carriage, held over the back, in both varieties.

Two examples of atypical tail carriage.

they are set well apart, their center on a line with the lowest point of the large, flaring ears and the base of the definite stop. Eyes can vary in color, as can pigment, according to the color of the barreled, and the brisket deep. The Chihuahua is slightly longer from the point of shoulder to the point of buttocks than it is in height at the withers, with somewhat shorter bodies seen on males.

A longhaired Chihuahua in full coat, magnificently groomed.

dog. The Chihuahua's saucy expression, once seen, can never be forgotten!

The head is set on a slightly arched, medium-length neck, sloping gracefully into well-laid back, lean shoulders. The topline is level, the ribs well-sprung but not

Although this is a tiny and dainty breed, the Chihuahua has muscular hindquarters, giving drive from behind and helping the dog to move with brisk, forceful action. A high-stepping or hackney action is not characteristic. The feet should turn neither in nor out, and, when viewed on the move, the legs should be neither too wide nor too close. Pasterns are flexible and the feet small and dainty; the toes are well divided but not spread.

The tail of the Chihuahua is rather special. It is of medium length, flattish in appearance, set high and carried up and over the back in sickle fashion. The American Kennel Club standard states that it is "carried sickle either up or out, or in a loop over the back, with tip just touching the back." Ideally it is flat, broadening slightly in the center and tapering to a point.

So, that is a general description of this enchanting little breed, but as we know, there are two coat types. The smooth variety has a soft-textured coat that is close and glossy. An undercoat and ruff is permissible in smooths. The hair on the tail should preferably be furry.

Long-coated Chihuahuas also have a soft-textured coat, which can be

For his size, the Chihuahua has good depth and breadth of chest.

The apple-domed skull, large eyes, flaring ears and short muzzle combine to give this "head breed" a most distinct look.

Chihuahua

A pup with clear eyes, beautiful coloration, a sparkling expression and a bright future!

either flat or slightly wavy. The coat should never be tight and curly, coarse or harsh to the touch. There is feathering on the ears, feet and legs, and there are "pants" on the hindquarters. A large ruff on the neck is desirable, and the tail is long and full, forming a plume. The coat is a double coat, meaning it has a soft dense undercoat beneath a harder outer coat (harder than cotton, but still soft!).

So now you know what the Chihuahua looks like, and you will probably be relieved to learn that color matters not one bit!

The Chihuahua has become popular around the world and, although breed standards vary between countries, breeders try to preserve the same basic type. This representative of the breed hails from Germany.

DESCRIPTION OF THE BREED

Overview

- The breed standard, approved by the Chihuahua Club of America and accepted by the American Kennel Club, describes the ideal Chihuahua, detailing physical conformation as well as character and movement.
- The head, a most prominent feature, has an apple-domed skull.
- The coat is seen in either the smooth or long-coated variety. There are no color restrictions placed on the breed.
- The tail is another special feature. It is flat, set high and carried sickle-like over the back. The tail on a longhaired Chihuahua is plumed.

Are You a Chihuahua Person?

You don't have to have big ears, and you can weigh more than just a few pounds, but you will need to be quick and alert to keep up with your Chihuahua!

You have chosen a pint-sized pet with an attitude that is bigger than life, and if you are not already an extrovert, you will find that your personality cannot help but grow with his.

You have chosen the smallest breed in the world, so if you want to tuck him into your pocket or carry him around in a tote bag, that's fine

This "littlest of guard dogs" patrols his territory with the best of them, possessing confidence and attitude way beyond his small size.

by him. However, you must remember that he is an active little creature, so don't let him leap out of your pocket onto the floor. He may think he's capable, but the floor's a long way down for someone so tiny.

You will find his diminutive size enormously convenient. If you travel around a lot, you can always fit him easily into a pet carrier. He is a great travel companion! He is tremendously loyal and always will want to be close to his owner, so you'd better accept that from the start. Your life won't be your own anymore, and there will be little privacy!

If you are going to be a really good Chihuahua owner, you will have to accept your dog's curiosity and his mischief. You will be expected to laugh with him in his games, and if he decides to tear a household bill to shreds, so much the better!

You might be the sort who enjoys taking your dog for walks, but of

The Chihuahua is an extroverted creature who's not shy about voicing his opinion.

Chihuahuas make wonderful pets for people who have the time and inclination to pamper their tiny pets. They are truly lap dogs extraordinaire who enjoy all of the comforts of home.

The most portable of breeds, Chihuahuas can easily be toted along to accompany their owners most anywhere.

course you will have to take care where you go, especially if there are sight-hounds around that might spot him from a distance and mistake him for a hare. Because he is so active, you will easily be able to exercise him in your own backyard, just as long as you keep him company and join in some of his games. He will love you enormously and will expect you to love him just as much in return.

Even if you live in an apartment, you are sure to find some space in there for your Chihuahua. In this case, you will obviously have to take him outdoors for additional exercise, and it's always safest to keep him on his lead when outside. Because Chihuahuas can rapidly lose body heat, if you live in a cold climate you will enjoy selecting several warm, attractive sweaters for your dog. Indeed, why not create his own miniature wardrobe?

If you have boisterous children in the family, then yours is probably not the right type of household for a Chihuahua. If you live alone and can spend most of your time doting on your pet, you are just the right owner. Some say that Chihuahuas are not dogs at all, but "four-legged babies." Now, what better baby could you possibly want? And if you decide to enlarge your family, why not just add another Chihuahua? That makes sense to me!

You will be able to keep yourself busy with a little "hairdressing" from time to time. Apart from regular grooming, a Chihuahua usually needs a bath about once a month, and the long-coated variety can certainly have one more frequently. This is a fun activity. You'll love it!

Lastly, if you are one of the sun-worshipers of the human species, you will

The ever-alert Chihuahua is in tune with his owner and environment. The only thing he doesn't seem to know is that he's a small dog!

have a willing canine companion to share your pleasure. There may not be enough sunshine in your yard for you to sit out, but if there is even the tiniest ray, you can be sure your Chihuahua will find it. Just take care that neither of you gets sunburn or sunstroke!

In short, your Chihuahua will give you oodles of love and attention, and you will only be the right owner if you are prepared to give just as much in return.

Sun-seekers will have a willing partner in the Chihuahua, but too much sun and heat are good for neither dog nor human! Keep your tiny companion's comfort and safety in mind when spending time outdoors.

ARE YOU A CHIHUAHUA PERSON?

Overview

- The Chihuahua person is ready to share all aspects of his life with his tiny and loyal companion. The Chihuahua needs an owner who enjoys spending time with his dog and will reciprocate the breed's devoted love.
- The Chihuahua person does not need a large living space to comfortably house a Chihuahua but must make provisions for the dog's outdoor exercise and housebreaking.
- The Chihuahua person has a canine companion that's easy to transport and will enjoy accompanying his owner whenever possible.
- The Chihuahua person makes certain that his dog is safe at all times.

Selecting a Chihuahua Breeder

As time has marched on, the Chihuahua has perhaps not grown in size but certainly has grown in popularity, so that now both the long- and smooth-coated varieties are known in most countries of the world. This means that there are a substantial number of Chihuahua breeders to choose from, but not every one is as good as the next. This is a pocket-sized dog, not expensive to feed and not requiring a great amount of space in which to live, and thus it might just appeal to the disreputable, profit-

Look for a breeder who comes highly recommended with an excellent reputation and who obviously loves the breed.

seeking breeders out there. If you have to wait for a puppy from the breeder of your choice, then wait. That time spent will be well worthwhile.

Prospective puppy-buyers should always keep foremost in their minds that there are many different kinds of breeder, some with the breed's best interest at heart, others less dedicated. It is essential that you locate one who not only has dogs you admire but also breeding ethics with which you can agree. Sadly, in all breeds, there are invariably some who are simply "in it for the money," and these you must give a wide berth.

Under no circumstances should you buy a puppy from a "puppy mill" or other third-party source, for in doing so you simply will be lining the pockets of such an unethical breeder. Ask yourself honestly, if you were a breeder, wouldn't you want to know exactly who was buying your carefully reared puppy? You would

When visiting a litter, you should see at least one of the parents. At least the mother should be on the premises, giving you a good idea of how the pups will mature in looks, health and temperament.

The breeder will likely have other adult Chihuahuas on the premises. Meet all of the breeder's dogs and observe his interactions with them.

not leave the matter simply in the hands of a dealer. The good breeder will interview potential owners to ensure that the pups go to good homes.

That said, there are many good breeders around and, if you look carefully, you will find just such a person. The AKC and Chihuahua Club of America are sources you can trust to provide contact information of reputable member breeders. You still need to meet these breeders to be sure that their standards of care are what you would expect. You must be sure that the breeder fully understands the breed and has given careful consideration to the way the Chihuahua has been bred, taking into consideration the health, soundness and pedigrees of his breeding stock.

The breeder you select should be someone who breeds from home, in which case the puppies will hopefully have been brought up in the house and will be familiar with all the activities and noises that surround them. It is unlikely to find a Chihuahua breeder who is housing all his dogs in a kennel environment. Small dogs don't do well in such an environment.

However large or small the breeding establishment, it is important that the conditions in which the puppies are raised are suitable. They should be clean, and the puppies should be well supervised in a suitable environment. All pups should look in tip-top condition and temperaments should be sound, the puppies full of fun with plenty of confidence.

The breeder should be perfectly willing to show you the dam, and it will be interesting for you to take careful note of her own temperament and how she

If you're interested in a show-quality Chihuahua, you must make this clear to the breeder when visiting the litter and take advice as to which pup shows the most promise.

CHAPTER 4

interacts with her offspring. If the dam is not available for you to see, be warned that this might be a sign that the puppy was not born on the premises, but has been brought in from elsewhere to be sold. This is far from ideal!

As for the stud dog, it is likely that he will not be available, for he may well be owned by someone else, and a careful breeder may have traveled hundreds of miles to use his stud services.

Nonetheless, dedicated breeders will at least be able to show you the sire's photo and pedigree, as well as tell you about him.

A well-chosen breeder will be able to give the new puppy owner much useful guidance, including advice about feeding. Some breeders give small quantities of food to the new owners when the puppies leave home, but in any event the breeder should always provide written details of exactly what type and quantity of food has been fed, and with what regularity, plus sugges- tions of how to change the diet as the

Seeing where the pups are raised is important. It is much better if they are kept inside, in the home with the family, rather than isolated in a kennel.

puppy matures. You will of course be able to make changes as time goes on, but they must be gradual.

A breeder will also need to tell you what vaccinations the puppy has received, if any, and any other relevant health documentation should be given to you at the time of purchase. Details about the puppy's worming routine must also be made clear. Many breeders also provide a health guarantee and/or temporary insurance for the puppy. This is an especially good idea and the new owner can subsequently decide whether or not to continue with this policy.

Quality pups come from quality parents. Good breeders make sure that each mating is planned to pass on only the best characteristics of the breed to each litter.

SELECTING A CHIHUAHUA BREEDER

Overview

- To find a reputable breeder, write, phone or email the American Kennel Club or the Chihuahua Club of America.
- Know what to expect from a breeder and be patient in your search.
- The breeder should be just as concerned with your suitability as an owner as you are with his suitability as a breeder.
- Ask about pedigrees, registration papers and references.
- The breeder should inform you about the incidence of hereditary conditions in his line and show you health clearances on the parents of the litter.

Finding the Right Puppy

When visiting a litter, watch the pups interact with each other and make sure that each and every puppy is healthy and sound, both physically and temperamentally.

W hen you have decided which breeders have the Chihuahuas you appreciate best, you will be anxious to visit litters of puppies that might be available. Many breeders allow people to view the puppies at about 5 or 6 weeks, but Chihuahuas usually don't move to their new homes until around 10 or 12 weeks of age. Chihuahuas, though devoted to their owners, can often be suspicious of those they don't know, so early socialization is of paramount importance.

A healthy puppy should strike you as being clean, without any sign of discharge from eyes or nose. His rear end should be spotless, with no sign of loose movements. Although any puppy's nails can be sharp, they should not be overly long, indicating that the breeder has clipped them as necessary.

All pups are irresistible, but remember to use your head, not just your heart, in selecting your puppy.

The coat should clearly be in excellent condition, not tacky, flaky or sparse in any way, and there should be absolutely no sign of parasites. Parasites such as fleas and lice cannot always be seen easily, but will be indicated by the puppy's scratching, and you might notice a rash.

Scratching, though, does not always mean that there is a parasitic or skin condition, for it can also be associated with teething. In this case, the puppy will only scratch around his head area. This will stop when the second set of teeth have come through and the gums are no longer sore.

Puppies should appear alert, inquisitive and expressive, all indicators of sound and typical temperament.

Take your time to meet all of the Chihuahuas on the breeder's premises. The adult dogs should respond to being handled just as the puppies should.

Scratching might also be connected with an ear infection, so a quick look inside your prospective puppy's ears will ensure that there is no build-up of wax, and there should be no odor from the ear. Of course, a good breeder will have checked that all puppies are in good health before offering them for sale.

Screening requirements may vary from country to country, but before purchasing your Chihuahua you should contact the breed club or the American Kennel Club to find out which genetic-health tests should have been done on the parents and pups. You must ask to see written proof of the test dates and results; do not just take the breeder's word for it.

Most puppies are outgoing and full of fun, so do not take pity on the overly shy one that hides away in a corner. Your chosen puppy should clearly enjoy your company when you come to visit, and this will make for a long-term bond between you. When you go to select your puppy, take with you the members of your immediate family with whom the puppy will spend time at home. It is essential that every family member agree with the important decision you are about to make, for a new puppy will inevitably change your lives.

Hopefully you did plenty of research about the breed long before reaching the decision to have a new puppy enter your lives. The Internet is a great source of information and you should buy some other books about the breed to keep along with this one for permanent ease of reference.

Breed clubs are also an important source of help and information. Some even publish their own leaflets and small booklets about the breed, and might even publish a book of champions so that you can see what your puppy's famous ancestors actually looked like. Look into some of the weekly

On his way to becoming a "couch potato"? If you allow him, your Chihuahua will gladly take a spot on your favorite chair—and there will be more than enough room for you to share!

CHAPTER 5

or monthly canine newspapers or magazines, all of which can be acquired through subscriptions. Most are not easily available at the local newsstand.

A word of caution to those who decide to look up breed information online. I urge you not to take all you read on the Internet as the absolute truth. These days anyone can set up a website and can write what they like, even though they may not have a sufficiently firm knowledge of the breed to do so. The Chihuahua Club of America (www.chihuahua-clubofamerica.com) and AKC (www.akc.org) are trusted sources of honest information.

Finally, it is a good idea to become a member of at least one breed club. In doing so, you will receive notification of breed-specific events in which you may like to participate, thus providing further opportunities to learn about the Chihuahua and meet people in the breed.

FINDING THE RIGHT PUPPY

Overview

- Visit the litter to see the puppies firsthand. You are seeking healthy, sound puppies. "Cute" is not a qualification, though bright eyes, shiny coats and alert temperaments count for a lot.
- Trust the breeder whom you've selected to sell you a healthy, genetically sound puppy that fits your lifestyle and personality.
- Do sufficient research on the breed before visiting the litter so that you know what to look for in a breeder and puppy, as well as what to expect when adding a Chihuahua to your family.
- If you intend to show, discuss this with the breeder.
- The breed club is a wonderful source of information; membership provides opportunity to become further involved in the breed.

CHAPTER 6

Welcoming the Chihuahua

Your Chihuahua puppy won't take up much space in your home, but everything must be exactly right. You will have lots of planning to do. He must have somewhere comfortable to sleep; safe, warm and away from drafts. Your yard or other exercise area must be absolutely secure. You will need to get some accessories for your puppy, and of course he will also need his own special food. Soon you will be able to collect your Chihuahua to bring home. For this momentous day, you will want to

Some Chihuahuas certainly ride in style! This "king of the road" has his own access door to the family's RV—now that's traveling!

be certain that everything at home is as well prepared as it can possibly be.

Hopefully you will have had an opportunity to see and select your puppy before the date of collection. Should this be the case, you will have had plenty of time to discuss with the breeder exactly what your puppy will need to make his life healthy, safe and enjoyable.

Your Chihuahua will certainly appreciate time in the yard to stretch his little legs. You'll need a securely fenced yard, free of pesticides, chemicals, poisonous plants and any other doggie dangers, to provide your dog with safe space outdoors.

Depending on where you live, you will probably have easy access to one of the large pet stores, or a good privately owned pet shop. If you can find a good shop owned by people who show their own dogs, they often have a wide range of specialty items and will probably be able to give sensible guidance as to what you need to buy. Major dog shows also usually have a variety of trade stands that cater to a dog's every need, and you are sure to be absolutely spoiled for choice!

How will other pets react to your Chihuahua? Maybe not at all! This Chihuahua is trying to get his Chessie housemate's attention, to no avail.

You will need some grooming equipment for your Chihuahua puppy, and you may need to add to this as your dog matures. At this early stage, a gentle brush and a small rubber curry comb will be your principal needs. You will also need canine nail clippers. You probably already have things like cotton balls and extra towels in stock as household items.

Where your puppy is to sleep will be a major consideration, and you should start as you mean to go on. It is only natural that the newcomer will be restless for the first couple of nights or so, but if you immediately take pity on the little soul and let him join you in your bedroom, he will expect to remain there always! Thus, it is essential that the bedding you choose should be eminently suitable, so that your puppy can rest as comfortably as possible in the intended place.

The choice of bedding for

Getting to know you! Chihuahuas get along well with other dogs and pets, provided they are introduced properly and allowed to become acquainted with each other.

your Chihuahua is very much a matter of personal preference, but most owners prefer to train their dogs in crates, as the crate has many benefits for housebreaking and general safety. Bear in mind that a puppy will not want a crate that is too large; a small-sized crate will suffice for the tiny Chihuahua as a puppy and adult.

wiser to choose a durable crate that can be washed or wiped down. This can easily be lined with comfortable soft bedding that can be washed frequently, for it is important that all of your dog's bedding is kept clean and dry. You should also choose a crate that is just slightly raised from the ground or otherwise positioned so that it will avoid drafts.

An important accessory is your Chihuahua's collar, to which you can attach his ID tags and his lead.

Wicker beds may look pretty, but they are dangerous because puppies chew them, and sharp wicker pieces can all too easily injure eyes or be chewed off and swallowed. It is

Although a Chihuahua is tiny, he can get into all kinds of mischief. Everyday household items may seem harmless enough, but a dainty cloth draped over the side of a little table full of fragile ornaments is merely tempting fate! Even more dangerous to a mischievous puppy are electric cables, so be sure they are concealed from his reach. Tiny teeth can bite through all too easily, causing what can be a fatal accident. Many cleaning them out of the way of your curious explorer. Antifreeze is especially dangerous; just a few drops can kill a small dog quickly.

When your puppy first arrives home, he is only natural that you will be proud and will want to show your new companion to your

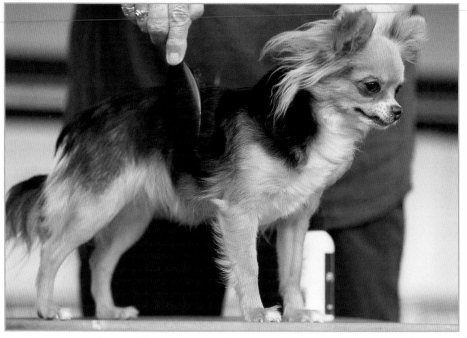

Accustom your Chihuahua to grooming by first getting him accustomed to standing still on the grooming table. This training will pay off for your Chihuahua's grooming sessions throughout his life.

agents, gardening aids and other household chemicals contain substances that are poisonous, so please keep friends. However, your puppy is making a big move in his short life, so the first two or three days are best spent quietly at home with you and your immediate family. When your puppy has found his feet and taken stock of his new surroundings, you will be able to introduce him to lots of new people. If you have young children, or if they visit, always carefully supervise any time spent with your young puppy. Youngsters can all too easily hurt a small puppy, even with the best of intentions, and the dainty Chihuahua is especially vunerable.

If your family has other pets, introductions should be

Your Chihuahua will take time to smell the flowers, but some can be toxic to dogs. Make sure no dangerous plants are growing or kept in areas to which the dog has access.

made slowly, and under close supervision. Most Chihuahuas get along well with other animals, but you should always exercise caution until you are certain that all concerned are going to be the best of friends.

WELCOMING THE CHIHUAHUA

Overview

- Go the pet store to get the essentials before your puppy comes home. You're going to need food, bowls, a collar and ID tags, toys, a leash and collar, a crate, a brush and comb and more.
- Make your home safe for your puppy by removing hazards from the dog's environment indoors and out.
- Socialization is critical to your puppy's proper development. Be proactive by introducing him to children and other dogs. Keep new experiences positive and fun.
- Give your pup time to get used to his new home before introducing different experiences.

Chihuahua Puppy Training

Your Chihuahua will usually be full of himself, and often even a little too "cock-sure." However, when he first arrives home, do not be surprised if he lacks a bit of confidence. Everything will be completely new to him. There will be no familiar sights and sounds, and even the smells around your home will be unfamiliar. It will be up to you to build up his confidence and give him the encouragement he will need during the early stages of training.

Begin by getting him used to the

Chihuahuas, being extremely intelligent dogs, are bright students and quick learners.

immediate members of your close family. Instilling confidence in your Chihuahua will help with his early socialization, and you will soon be able to introduce him to your wider family and friends. Please try not to bombard him with too many new people and situations all at the same time, as he will be overwhelmed.

Depending on the age of your puppy, and whether his course of vaccinations is complete, you may or may not be able to take him out in public places immediately. Whichever the case, I would still advise you to allow him to settle down at home for the first few days before venturing further. There will be lots you can do with your Chihuahua puppy at home, so you will both undoubtedly have great fun, but please allow him to get sufficient rest, too.

If restricted to your home territory for a little while, you can play games with him using suitably safe, soft toys,

Some owners prefer the nylon harness to the traditional collar, feeling that the harness is more comfortable for small dogs.

The sit command is an easy exercise and a good place to begin your Chihuahua's obedience training.

but do not allow him to tug on anything too strongly. Check regularly that sharp or unsafe parts, such as squeakers, do not become detached from the toy. These can cause injury, and your puppy's teeth will be very sharp, so toys can easily be damaged.

Whether or not you plan to show your Chihuahua, it is always good to do a little early training, getting him to stand calmly on a table and to be gently groomed. Both will be helpful on numerous occasions, including visits to the vet, when it is much easier to deal with a well-behaved dog. You will be so proud of your clever companion!

Accustom your puppy to being on a lead, which is always a strange experience for a tiny youngster. Begin by just attaching a simple collar, not too tightly, but not so loosely that he can squirm out of it or that it can be caught on things, causing panic and possible injury. Just put it on

for a few minutes at a time, lengthening each period slightly until your puppy feels comfortable in his first item of "clothing." Don't expect miracles; this may take a few days.

Then, when he is comfortable in the collar, attach a small lightweight lead. The one you select must have a secure catch, yet be simple to attach and release as necessary. Until now, your puppy has simply gone where he has pleased and will find it very strange to be attached to someone restricting his movements. For this reason, when training my own puppies, I like to allow them to "take" me for the first few sessions. I then start to exert a little pressure, and soon enough training can start in earnest, with the puppy coming with me as I lead the way. It is usual to begin training the puppy to walk on your left-hand side. When this has been accomplished to

Your Chihuahua pup is looking up to you—with his big eyes—to provide him with good care, safety and education.

your satisfaction, you can try moving him on your right, but there is absolutely no hurry. If you plan to show your Chihuahua, you will generally move your dog on your left, but there are occasions when it is necessary also to move him on your right so as not to obstruct the judge's view.

As your puppy gets older, you can teach him to sit, always using a simple one-

succeed. Always give plenty of praise when appropriate. *Never* shout or get angry when your dog does not achieve your aim, for this will do more harm than good. If yours is destined to be a show dog, you may decide not to teach "sit," as in the show ring he will be expected to stand.

When your Chihuahua puppy can venture out to public places, begin by taking

Here's an instance in which crate training comes in handy as these Chihuahuas wait for their turn in the show ring.

word command, "Sit," while exerting gentle pressure on his rump to show him what you expect. This will take a little time, but you will soon

him somewhere quiet without too many distractions. Soon you will find his confidence increasing and you can then introduce him to new places,

A handful to train! During training, you may have to guide your pup into the position you want him to assume until he gets the idea.

with exciting sights, sounds and smells. He must always be on a safe lead that cannot be slipped (quite different from the type used in the show ring). When you have total confidence in one another, you may be able to let him off-lead, but always keep him in sight. Be absolutely sure the place you have chosen for off-lead exercise is utterly safe and securely enclosed, and that no strange dogs can suddenly appear from "nowhere."

You will need to train your puppy to stay in his crate

Because of their tiny size, Chihuahuas only require lightweight collars and leads.

when required; this is recommended for both show and pet dogs. At shows in most countries, Toy breeds are housed in crates for at least part of the time while not actually being exhibited in the ring. Crates are useful for safety while traveling and, if used in the home, most dogs seem to look upon them as a safe place to go and don't mind staying in their crates for short periods. This is useful for safe confinement whenever the need arises.

When you commence crate-training, remain within sight of your dog and give him a toy or treat to occupy his mind.

To begin, leave him in the crate for very short spells of just a minute or two, then gradually build up the timespan. However, never confine a dog to a crate for too long, for this would be unkind. Always spend some time with him, playing or just petting him, after time in the crate.

CHIHUAHUA PUPPY TRAINING

Overview

- When he first comes home, he will need some time to adjust and some encouragement from you to build up his inherent confidence.
- Start with introductions to the family, then progress to other people, other dogs and new places once your pup has received the proper vaccinations and can go out in public.
- Choose safe toys for your Chihuahua and engage him in play.
- Standing on a grooming table, wearing his collar and lead and practicing basic exercises like "sit" should be introduced and taught with lots of praise.
- Learn the principles of successful puppy training.
- Your Chihuahua's crate is a valuable tool for giving him a place of his own and keeping him safe in many situtations.

House-training Your Chihuahua

Initially it might be difficult to accept that your tiny bundle of fun could ever be naughty, but I can assure you that he will! There will be times when you have to admonish him, but of course this must always be done gently and when there is good reason. Your Chihuahua is intelligent and very cute, and he will likely know when he has done wrong. Training will be a very important part of your routine from day one. To house-train with success, you will need to be firm, but never harsh, and you must certainly never be rough

A big part of dog training is toilet training! Teaching the dog polite potty habits is essential to a happy and clean relationship with your Chihuahua.

with your Chihuahua.

When your puppy first arrives in your home, he may or may not already be house-trained, albeit to a limited extent. However, you must always realize that your home is completely different from the breeder's, so he will have to re-learn the house rules. Doors will not be located in the same places, your family may go to bed and rise at different times and it will un-doubtedly take him a little time to learn and to adapt.

The speed of your house-training success will depend to a certain extent on your own environment and on the season of the year. Most puppies are perfectly happy to go out into the yard in dry weather, but when rain is pouring down, many feel rather differently and will need considerable encouragement!

Paper training is always useful in the very early stages of training. This

The nose knows! Dogs learn much by sniffing, such as how to locate their relief area and if other dogs have been there. The dog's sense of smell is a key to training him to a specific spot for toileting.

When housebreaking your dog, always lead him to his area on his leash. If you don't have a fenced yard, you will have to take your Chihuahua out for walks to do his business.

should be placed by the door so that the dog learns to associate the paper with the exit to the wide world outside. When he uses the paper, he should be praised. Obviously it is ideal if the puppy can be let out as soon as he shows any sign of wanting to do his toilet, but again this may depend on whether your home has immediate access to the yard and whether or not his course of vaccinations is complete.

Remember that puppies need to relieve themselves much more frequently than adult animals, certainly immediately after waking and following meals. In fact, taking your pup outside every hour while he is awake is not a bad idea at all. Always keep both eyes and ears open, for a youngster will not be able to wait those extra two or three minutes until it is convenient for you to let him out. If you delay, accidents will certainly happen, so be warned!

As your puppy matures, "asking" to be let out when necessary will become second nature, and it will be rare if you have

The crate is an invaluable tool for a dog's training and safety. It can be used wherever you go, as your Chihuahua's small crate is easy to bring along.

Accustoming your Chihuahua to a crate at home will come in handy in other situations such as at the vet's, traveling to a show, waiting at the groomer's, etc.

CHAPTER 8

You choose your dog's relief site and train him to use it, so it's best to pick an out-of-the-way spot in the yard rather than your flower garden!

a Chihuahua that is unclean in the house. A stud dog, however, can be different, for he may well want to mark his territory, and your table and chair legs may be just the places he decides to choose!

Simple word commands are very helpful, "Potty"

being my own favorite, and it seems to work. Never, ever forget to give praise when the deed is done in the desired place. However, if an accident happens, you should indeed give a verbal reprimand, but this will only work if your Chihuahua is caught in the act. If you try to reprimand him after the event, he will simply not know what he has done wrong and this will only serve to confuse.

It is essential that any mess be cleaned up immediately. If a dog has done his toilet in the wrong place, it must be cleaned thoroughly so as to disguise the smell. If he can smell it, he will want to use that particular place again. When your puppy is old enough to be exercised in public places, always carry with you a "pooper scoop" or small plastic bag so that any droppings can be removed. The anti-dog lobby exists in every country, so please give them no cause for complaint!

HOUSE-TRAINING YOUR CHIHUAHUA

Overview

- The first hurdle for all puppy owners is housebreaking, teaching the dog clean indoor behavior.
- Bring your puppy out frequently and learn to recognize his signs that he needs "to go."
- Teach a relief command so that your puppy will be encouraged to eliminate when you've brought him outside.
- Paper training is an option for getting started; soon your pup will learn that outdoors is the place to go to relieve himself.
- Be clean! Always clean up any accidents indoors right away, and pick up any droppings in your yard or in public.

CHAPTER 9

Teaching Basic Commands

Your Chihuahua puppy is alert and intelligent, and thus is perfectly capable of learning, just as long as you are consistent in your training. Be gentle in your approach and he will be glad to please you, especially if he can see the purpose in what he is doing. All dogs like to have a reason for doing the things that their owners tell them. Just remember that he does not only have a saucy expression but also lots of spirit. Some say he possesses "terrier-like" qualities, so if you do not keep on top of his training, he could just get away with murder!

A little push on the rump and voila! A successful sit.

Although some show dogs are trained in obedience, many exhibitors feel this can be detrimental to a dog's performance in the show ring, so consider this if you plan to show. Nonetheless, every dog must be taught the basic commands and good manners.

The sit/stay is accomplished by using a combination of hand signals and verbal commands, moving farther from the dog a little at a time.

In all training, it is essential to get your dog's full attention, which many owners do with the aid of treats so that the dog learns to associate treats with praise. The following training method involves using food treats, although you will wean your dog off these training aids in time so that your training is based on praise with an occasional food reward. Always use very simple commands, just one or two short words, and keep sessions short so they do not become boring for your dog. Hold your training sessions in a securely enclosed area.

The down exercise is not always the easiest for dogs to learn, but a treat as motivation certainly helps the process along.

SIT COMMAND

With the lead in your left-hand, hold a small treat in your right, letting your dog smell or lick the treat but not take it. Move it away as you say "Sit," your hand rising slowly over the dog's head so that he looks upward. In doing so he will bend his knees and will sit. When this has been accomplished, give the treat and lavish praise.

HEEL COMMAND

A dog trained to heel will walk alongside his handler without pulling. Again, the lead should be held in your left hand while the dog assumes the sit position next to your left leg. Hold the end of the lead in your right hand, but also control it lower down with your left.

Step forward with your right foot, saying the word "Heel." To begin, just take three steps, then command him to sit again. Repeat this procedure until he carries out the task without pulling. Then you can increase the number of strides to five, seven and so on. Give verbal praise at the close of each section of the exercise, and at the end of the training session let him enjoy himself with a free run and some playtime.

DOWN COMMAND

When your dog is proficient in sitting, you can introduce the word "Down." First, it is essential to understand that a dog will consider the down position as a submissive one, so gentle training is important in teaching this command.

With your Chihuahua sitting by your left leg, in the sit position, hold the lead in your left hand and a treat in your right. Place your left hand on top of the dog's shoulders (without pushing) and hold the treat under his nose, saying "Down" in a quiet tone of voice. Gradually move the treat along the floor, in front of the dog, all the while talking gently. He will follow the treat, lowering himself down. When his elbows touch the floor, you can release the treat and give praise, but try to get him to remain there for a few seconds before getting up. Gradually the time of the down exercise can be increased.

STAY COMMAND

Stay can be taught with your dog either in a sit or in a down position, as usual with the lead in your left hand and the treat in your right. Allow him to lick the treat as you say "Stay" while standing directly in front of the dog, having moved from your position beside him. Silently count to about five, then move back to your original position alongside him, allowing your dog to have the treat while giving him lavish praise.

Keep practicing "stay" just as described for a few days, then gradually increase the distance between you, using your hand with the palm

With Toy and other small breeds, it's necessary to crouch down to the dog's level while training so as to have better control and not to intimidate the dog.

facing the dog, as an indication that he must stay. Soon you should be able to do this exercise without a lead, and your Chihuahua will increasingly stay for longer periods of time. Always give lavish praise upon completion of the exercise.

Chihuahuas are natural showmen and will delight in doing tricks like dancing on their hind legs for a treat.

CHAPTER 9

COME COMMAND

Your Chihuahua will love to come back to you when called. The idea is to invite him to return, always giving a treat and lots of praise when he does. Never call him to scold him; coming to you must always be positive. It is important for the dog to learn to come reliably, for this should bring him running back to you if ever he is in danger or moving out of sight. Always take special care not to call your dog when he could run into danger, like passing traffic.

A flexible lead can be used with a reliably heel-trained Chihuahua. It's a safe way to gve the dog a broader area to explore, while it retracts when you need to keep your dog close.

TRICKS

The Chihuahua is truly a charming little character and may well enjoy learning a trick or two. What you teach, if anything at all, will be very much a matter of choice, but some dogs learn to offer their paw, and others like to sit up and "beg," which is particularly enchanting.

TEACHING BASIC COMMANDS

Overview

- Begin basic obedience training on the right paw: select a quiet and secure environment, keep lessons short and positive and use treats and praise for motivation and rewards.
- Get your puppy's attention and maintain it.
- The basic commands include come, sit, stay, down and heel.
- Crouch down to your Chihuahua's level when introducing commands and guiding him into positions.
- Practice with your Chihuahua daily so that he becomes consistent 100% of the time.
- Have a little fun and teach your Chihuahua a trick or two.

CHAPTER 10

Home Care for Your Chihuahua

B ecause you love your Chihuahua, you will want to keep him in the best of health throughout his long life, which is often around 15 or 16 years, sometimes even more. Over the years you will have grown to know your pet, just as you would a child, so you will know when he is feeling unwell.

Knowing your dog will help you to recognize problems so that you can take your pet to the vet without delay for further investigation.

If your Chihuahua ever seems a little "off," not as active and personable as usual, this could indicate a health problem and warrants a call to the vet.

DENTAL CARE

Keeping teeth in good condition is your responsibility. You owe this to your dog, for dental problems do not stop inside the mouth. When gums are infected, all sorts of health problems can subsequently arise, spreading through the dog's system and possibly leading even to death. Toy dogs can be especially prone to dental problems.

Rope toys are safe chews that act like dental floss, getting in between the teeth as the dog chews.

You may clean your Chihuahua's teeth extremely gently and carefully, using a very small toothbrush and special canine toothpaste. Take particular care if any of the teeth are beginning to loosen. Your dog may not like this procedure much at first, but should easily get used to it if you clean regularly. Experienced breeders sometimes use a special dental scraper, but damage can be done with this, especially on a Toy breed, so I do

A trio of happy travelers! Chihuahua owners love to make their dogs part of their lives wherever they go and whatever they do.

not recommend it for use by the average pet owner.

When cleaning the teeth, always check the gums for signs of inflammation. If you notice that the gums look red or swollen, a visit to your vet would be worthwhile.

FIRST AID

Accidents can happen and, if they do, you must remain as cool, calm and collected as possible so that you can help your Chihuahua.

Insect stings are quite common. If it is still there, the "stinger" should be removed with tweezers. Ice can be applied to reduce the swelling and an accurate dosage (ask your vet!) of antihistamine can be given. If a sting is inside the mouth, consult your vet at once.

Accidental poisoning is also a worry, as dogs can investigate all sorts of things, not all of which are safe. If you suspect poisoning, try to ascertain the cause, because

The delectable, collectible Chihuahua! Who can stop at just one?

treatment may vary according to the type of poison ingested. Vomiting or sudden bleeding from an exit point, such as the gums, can be indications of poisoning. Urgent veterinary attention is essential.

Small abrasions should be cleaned thoroughly and antiseptic applied. In the case of serious bleeding, initially apply pressure above the area. For minor burns, apply cool water.

In the case of shock, such as following a car accident, keep the dog warm while veterinary aid is sought as quickly as possible.

For heat stroke, cold water must be applied immediately, especially over the shoulders. In severe cases, the dog should be submerged in water up to his neck if possible. Dogs can die quickly from heat stroke, so urgent veterinary attention is of paramount importance. Conversely, in the case of hypothermia, keep the dog warm with hot-water bottles and give a warm bath if possible while you call the vet.

HOME CARE FOR YOUR CHIHUAHUA

Overview

- Know the signs of wellness so that you can recognize when your Chihuahua's health may be compromised by disease.
- Dental care is an important part of every Toy-dog owner's home-care routine for his dog. Brush your Chihuahua's teeth carefully and regularly, keeping an eye out for any signs of trouble.
- Acquaint yourself with symptoms of problems and basic first-aid techniques. Stay calm while administering first aid and seek veterinary aid as soon as possible.

Feeding Your Chihuahua

Because your Chihuahua is so small, it will be easy to notice if you are allowing him to put on too many extra pounds, or should I say ounces? An overweight dog is more prone to health problems than one of the correct weight for his size. Not only will there be additional strain on the heart and joints, but also the likelihood of extra risk under anesthesia.

If you feed dry foods, it is important to select one described by the manufacturer as "small bite" size, rather than feeding large kibble

"Food! I'm getting hungry just thinking about it!"

designed for an Irish Wolfhound!

Today there is an enormous range of specially prepared foods available for dogs, many of them scientifically balanced and suitable for specific age ranges. It is really a matter of personal preference as to which particular food you decide to use,

There is no better food for puppies than their mother's milk for the first weeks of life.

though initially you will undoubtedly be influenced by the brand and type of food that has been fed to your new puppy by his breeder. Changes can, of course, be made to his diet, but never change suddenly from one food to another or your Chihuahua is likely to get an upset tummy. Introduce a new brand of food gradually over a few days until the old brand is phased out. There is usually no harm at all in changing the flavor of food, while keeping with the same brand. This can add some variety to the diet, or you might prefer to add a little

Chihuahuas can become fussy eaters if given the opportunity. Be sensible when selecting your dog's food.

flavored stock to tempt the palate.

Should you decide to feed a dry product, be sure to thoroughly read the feeding instructions. Some dry foods need to be moistened, especially those for young-sters. Dry food should also be stored carefully, bearing in mind that its vitamin value declines if not used fairly quickly, usually within about three months. It is essential that a plentiful supply of fresh water is available for your dog, especially when feeding dry foods, though dogs should of course have access to water at all times.

Because of the enormous range of products available, you may find it difficult to choose without advice from an experienced Chihuahua person. Keep in mind that in adulthood, an active dog will require a higher protein content than one that lives a sedate life. No dog should be fed chocolate of the kind that humans eat, as this is poisonous to dogs. Onions also are toxic to dogs.

Some owners prefer to feed fresh foods. In this case, they should be absolutely certain that they are feeding a well-balanced diet and that no dangerous things like cooked chicken bones are included in the meals. There are many proponents of the raw-food, more natural diet of the wild. Interested owners should educate themselves about how to properly prepare a fresh-food diet to provide complete and balanced nutrition. Cooked vegetables are also beneficial to this type of diet.

Many owners are tempted to feed tidbits between meals, but this is not a good idea, as the weight can pile on almost imperceptibly. A very suitable alternative is to give the occasional piece of carrot. Most dogs love them! Carrots don't put on any weight, and are a useful aid to keeping the teeth clean.

Don't forget the water! Water is important for your dog at all times, so always bring some along wherever you go.

Chihuahua

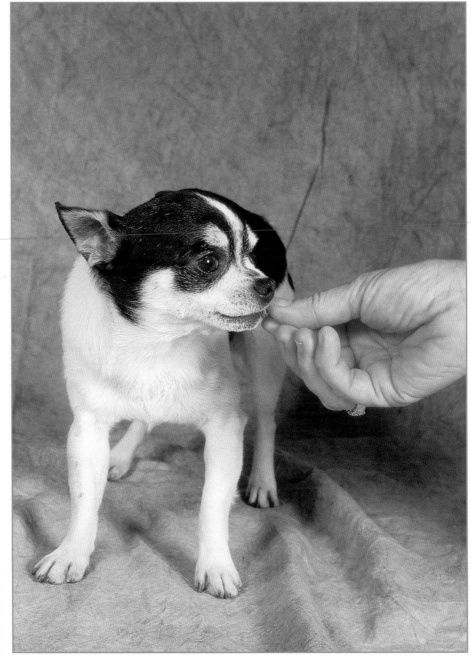

All dogs respond to a tasty tidbit! Remember, though, that you can quickly overdo it with a tiny Chihuahua if he is given too many treats in addition to his meals.

How many times a day you feed your adult Chihuahua will likely depend on personal preference and the family's schedule, but most tend to feed two meals a day. Some even feed three smaller ones. Puppies need to be fed more frequently than adults, and your breeder can give you good advice about changes in feeding schedule and the transition from puppy food to adult food.

As a dog gets older, his metabolism changes, so feeding requirements may change as well. This can include modifying portions and the feeding schedule, and possibly switching to a senior-dog food. By then, of course, you will know your pet well, and should be able to adjust feeding accordingly. If you have any queries, your vet will be able to guide you in the right direction.

You do not need large bowls for your Chihuahua, but make sure thay are made of a durable material and are easy to clean.

FEEDING YOUR CHIHUAHUA

Overview

- Quality counts when feeding the Chihuahua. Offering a complete, balanced dog food is the most reliable and convenient way to provide optimal nutrition for your dog.
- Discuss with your vet and/or breeder the feeding schedule and the amount to feed your Chihuahua at his various stages of life.
- Pick a "small-bite" food for your tiny Chihuahua.
- Avoid too many treats, as this can quickly lead to obesity.
- Educate yourself about nutrition if you choose to prepare your dog's diet yourself.
- Your Chihuahua's health relies upon a proper diet.

Grooming Your Chihuahua

W hether you have a smooth- or long-coated Chihuahua, grooming will be minimal compared with that of many other breeds.

Compare your own long-coated dog with an Afghan Hound, and you will realize how lucky you are! I say lucky, but most owners take great pleasure in grooming, and certainly this pleasure is shared by the dog, provided he is not allowed to get into an unkempt state.

Ideally your Chihuahua will be groomed on a firm table with a non-

Longhaired Chihuahuas will require more grooming than their smooth counterparts, something an owner should consider when first obtaining a Chihuahua.

slip surface. You will find that Chihuahua owners use slightly different pieces of equipment, according to what they find suits best. You will hopefully get good advice from the breeder about grooming when you discuss buying your new puppy, but doubtless you will settle into your own routine rather quickly.

Long grass is cool to lie in on a hot day, but can also introduce your dog to insects, allergens and other irritants. Use grooming time as time to inspect your dog's skin and coat for any signs of problems.

COAT CARE

However frequently you choose to bathe your Chihuahua, it is essential to keep the coat clean and to groom regularly. It is always wise to check the coat every day so that no unexpected problems start to build up. Long-coated Chihuahuas are not especially prone to knots and tangles, but regular brushing is necessary to take out any loose hair.

A soft bristle brush is an essential piece of equipment, and some like to use a small rubber curry comb to help massage and stimulate the skin.

Regular grooming keeps your Chihuahua as fresh as a flower!

Even massaging with your hand in the direction of coat growth helps to keep the coat glossy.

On smooths, some people like to use a chamois leather or piece of velvet for the finishing touch. There are grooming mitts made to fit on the hand, soft leather on one side and velvet on the other. These can be most useful for smooths.

Tear staining can be a problem in Chihuahuas. A smear of protective grease under the eye can help to minimize this, and it serves to protect the skin. Tear stains can be gently wiped away with a cleansing product and soft cotton.

BATHING YOUR CHIHUAHUA
Some Chihuahua owners who exhibit their dogs like to bathe them prior to each show, especially if they have long coats. Others choose to bathe less frequently. In any event, a quick bath about once a month is a good idea. A Chihuahua is small enough to bathe in the sink if you prefer not to use the bathtub. If a Chihuahua puppy is accustomed to being bathed from a young age, he will be perfectly happy to accept this part of the grooming procedure as he grows older.

Always brush your Chihuahua's coat thoroughly before bathing, then stand your dog on a non-slip surface and test the water temperature on the back of your hand. Use a canine shampoo, not a human one, taking care not to get water into the eyes and ears. It is usually wise to wash the head last so that shampoo does not drip into the eyes while you are concentrating on another part of the body. Take care to reach all the slightly awkward places so that no area is neglected.

Carefully lift your Chihuahua out of the sink or bath wrapped in a warm, clean towel. Then dry your

A grooming table makes grooming time easier for dog and owner. The dog is trained to stand still on the table for his beauty sessions, and the table raises the dog to a more comfortable height for you.

Chihuahua

Two of the breed's hallmarks, large eyes and large ears, need special care and attention. Removing tear stains, cleaning the ears and inspecting both the ears and the eyes for good health must be part of your grooming routine.

Chihuahua using a small blow dryer on the lowest heat, or even keep your dog in front of a gentle fan heater to benefit from its warm air, remembering that many dogs do not like air blowing towards their faces. Keep him indoors, away from drafts, until his coat is completely dry.

EARS AND EYES

It is important to keep your Chihuahua's eyes and ears clean. Eyes are especially liable to get dust and debris in them because the dog is so low to the ground. The eye area should be carefully wiped, perhaps using one of the special cleaners available from good pet stores.

At any sign of injury to the eye, or if the eye turns blue, veterinary attention must be sought immediately. If an eye injury is dealt with quickly, it can often be repaired; if neglected, it can lead to loss of sight.

If your dog has been shaking his head or scratching at his ears, there may well be an infection or ear mites. A thick brown discharge and malodorous smell are also indicative of these problems, so veterinary consultation is needed right away.

If you have a smooth, you should pay special attention to the ears, for they can get greasy. This causes the hair to fall out so that the leathers are left bare. Different people have different remedies, but a mild anti-bacterial soap is one option. When the ear is dry, it should be brushed daily with a very soft baby brush until the hair grows back in again.

NAILS AND FEET

Nails must always be kept trimmed, but how frequently they need clipping depends very much on the surface upon which your dogs walks. Those living their lives primarily on carpets or on grass will need more frequent attention to their nails than

Chihuahua

Your pet shop should carry special nail clippers made for dogs, which enable you to cut your dog's nails with minimal fuss. Nail clipping is not often an enjoyable experience for a dog, so you want to make his pedicures painless!

those who regularly move on a hard surface.

Your Chihuahua should be trained to accept nail clipping from an early age. Take great care not to cut into the quick, the blood vessel that runs through the nail, for this is painful. It is a good idea to keep a styptic pencil or some styptic powder on hand to stop the bleeding in case of an accident. Cutting just a small sliver of nail at a time is the safest approach. You should also inspect feet regularly to be sure that nothing has become wedged or embedded between the pads.

ANAL GLANDS

A dog's anal glands are located on either side of the anal opening. Sometimes these become blocked and require evacuation. Experienced breeders often do this themselves, but pet owners would be well advised to leave this to their vet. Firm stools help to evacuate the anal glands naturally. Don't include too much meat in your Chihuahua's diet, for this can cause stools to be soft and black, and may even lead to painful anal ulcers.

GROOMING YOUR CHIHUAHUA

Overview

- While neither variety of Chihuahua requires extensive grooming, proper coat maintenance is a vital part of his overall health-care program and must be initiated when the pup is young.
- The Chihuahua owner must tend to his dog's coat as well as his nails, ears, eyes and anal sacs.
- Owners of pet Chihuahuas usually bathe their dogs about once a month.
- When dealing with ear or eye problems, owners must not wait too long to seek treatment. Timely veterinary attention can mean the difference between an easily treatable condition and permanent damage.

CHIHUAHUA

Keeping the Chihuahua Active

The Chihuahua, like any other dog, loves to investigate new places and new smells. This keeps his senses alert, and probably gives him wonderful things to dream about when, in his active day, he finds a moment to slumber. Physical exercise also provides stimulation for the brain. Even though a Chihuahua is smaller than other breeds, he requires his exercise just like everyone else. Some Chihuahuas, when trained,

Your Chihuahua's favorite activities are anything he can do with his owner. He's a fun and active companion packed into a handy small size.

are fairly obedient when off-lead, but you must keep foremost in your mind that this is the tiniest of breeds. Accidents can happen all too easily when larger, heavier dogs are encoun- tered. This is especially so if your Chihuahua decides to stand his ground, which you can be pretty certain he will! Unless your Chihuahua is used to children, he might also take exception to toddlers approaching him unexpectedly, so you must keep your wits about you when out walking. It's safest to keep him on-lead in public. It is also important that your Chihuahua is not left damp following exercise in inclement weather.

Toys for Toys! Safe toys of appropriate size for extra-small dogs will definitely be appreciated.

If you have more than one Chihuahua, they will provide each other with exercise by playing together. If yours is an only pet, you will be your Chihuahua's exercise partner. Lots of fun and amusement can be found around your house and yard.

A wire pen, known as an "ex- pen," is useful for giving dogs an area of safe confinement outdoors.

Chihuahua

There are many activities to keep the Chihuahua mentally stimulated. For

Chihuahuas are capable of success in agility trials, provided that the competitions accommodate small breeds.

example, Chihuahuas are now used in therapy work, visiting nursing homes and hospitals to cheer people up with a friendly snuggle. The breed's small size and outgoing nature make the visit something to which hospital patients and the elderly greatly look forward. It is also not unknown for a Chihuahua to become a "hearing dog." This is a dog that is specially trained to

Chihuahuas are excellent at hearing-dog work, acting as assistants for people with hearing deficiencies.

listen for sounds like telephones and doorbells ringing and kettles whistling, things of great assistance to an owner with impaired hearing.

In some countries Chihuahuas even take part in obedience trials, though it has to be said that the Chihuahua is not a breed that springs immediately to mind when one thinks of agility trials. Golden Retrievers and Border Collies

seem to be more inclined than our saucy housemate. The Toy breeds, like the Chihuahua, can compete in agility; of course, all of the obstacles are smaller in size. No matter how talented our Chihuahuas are, they will never outrun a Border Collie around the course.

Even if your Chihuahua does not take part in any of these activities, you can enjoy endless hours of fun together. He thrives on time spent with you and will love games with suitably safe toys. Those designed for dogs

to tug are not right for Chihuahuas, for they may loosen those little teeth. Always check toys regularly to ensure that no loose parts might cause accidental damage.

Rope toys can provide safe chewing but should never be used for pulling and tug-of-war games.

KEEPING THE CHIHUAHUA ACTIVE

Overview

- Exercise for the Chihuahua provides both physical and mental stimulation.
- It is best to keep your Chihuahua on-lead when walking out in public. Always keep your tiny friend's safety foremost in your mind.
- Consider therapy work to keep your dog active and bring happiness to others.
- Chihuahuas can be trained for assistance work.
- Despite his size, the Chihuahua can compete in obedience and agility.
- The best way to keep your Chihuahua active is to participate in activities together.

CHAPTER 14

Your Chihuahua and His Vet

One of the conveniences of having a Chihuahua is his size, and this can be particularly useful when visiting your vet. Your pet can sit easily on your lap, or in a lightweight carrying case or his small crate, provided he is completely at ease being thus transported. Any of these methods will help to protect him from the unwanted attentions of bigger dogs, for he may be feeling a little off-color and would appreciate a little peace and quiet.

It is sensible to make early contact with your vet, in part to build up

Show your Chihuahua how much you love him by being vigilant about his veterinary care.

rapport for any consequent visits. Obviously if your puppy's course of vaccinations is not yet complete, you will need to take him to the vet in any case, but it is wise take him for a complete check-up soon after bringing him home.

Trips to the vet are easy with the tiny, transportable Chihuahua.

If you do not already have a vet for other family pets, you should select your vet carefully. Preferably take recommendations from your breeder or another dog owner whose opinion you trust. Location is also an important factor, for you must be able to get your dog to the vet quickly in an emergency and the vet must be able to respond rapidly when needed. If you live in a rural area, please be sure that you choose a vet who has plenty of dealings with small animals. Many have a great deal of experience with farm animals, but sadly their experience with dogs is limited, something some owners have learned to their regret in the past.

Every dog (and every person, too) requires regular check-ups. Discuss the frequency of visits with your veterinarian.

VACCINATIONS

Routine vaccinations vary slightly depending upon the area in which you live and the type of vaccine used by your particular vet. Your vet will advise you exactly about timing, when your dog can be exercised in public places after the course is complete and when boosters are due. Many vets now send reminder notices for boosters, but you should still make a note on your calendar. If booster shots are overdue, it will probably be necessary to give the full vaccination program again. If you are visiting your vet for an initial vaccination program, do not allow your dog to come into close contact with other dogs in the waiting room, nor indeed the waiting room floor!

Some people prefer not to subject their animals to routine vaccinations, but opt for homeopathic alternatives. This needs to be carried out to the letter, so you must be educated and be guided be a vet who also practices homeopathy. Also bear in mind that it will probably be difficult to find a boarding kennel that accepts a dog without proof of a routine vaccination program. You must also adhere to local ordinances regarding certain vaccinations such as rabies.

PREVENTATIVE CARE

If your puppy has been bought from a truly dedicated breeder, all necessary care will have been provided not only for the litter but also for the dam. She will have had regular health checks and boosters, with a worming routine. These will stand her puppies in good stead and provide them with greater immunity than would otherwise be the case.

It is also of great importance that any recommended tests for genetic abnormalities were carried out prior to the mating. A genuinely caring and ethical breeder will only have bred from a sound,

Check your
Chihuahua's
teeth and
make sure
that dental
exams are
part of his
check-ups.
Toy breeds
are prone to
problems with
their teeth.

healthy bitch and will have selected a stud dog of similar quality.

CHECK-UPS

When your Chihuahua goes along to the vet for booster vaccinations, your vet will also give him a brief routine health check. If the vet you use does not do this as a matter of course, request that he check your dog's heart during your visit, especially if your dog is past middle age.

NEUTERING AND SPAYING

Whether or not you decide to have your dog spayed is a matter of personal choice, but something I would never choose unless illness necessitated it. In any event, please never allow a vet to spay your bitch until after her first season. Timing "mid-season" will usually be advised.

Should you decide to opt for neutering your male dog or spaying your bitch, you will have to take special care with subsequent weight control. In some cases, an aggressive or over-dominant male can be easier to cope with after neutering, but this is by no means always so.

Obviously there are some reasons of ill health that necessitate such operations, particularly pyometra, which will usually require a bitch's ovaries to be removed. In the case of a male with only one or neither testicle descended into the scrotum, your vet may well advise castration to prevent the likelihood of cancer. Chihuahuas are sensitive to anesthesia. Discuss this with your vet.

RECOGNIZING THE SYMPTOMS

If you love your Chihuahua and you spend plenty of time together, you will know when something is amiss. He may go off his food or seem dull and listless. His eyes, usually bright and alive, may seem to

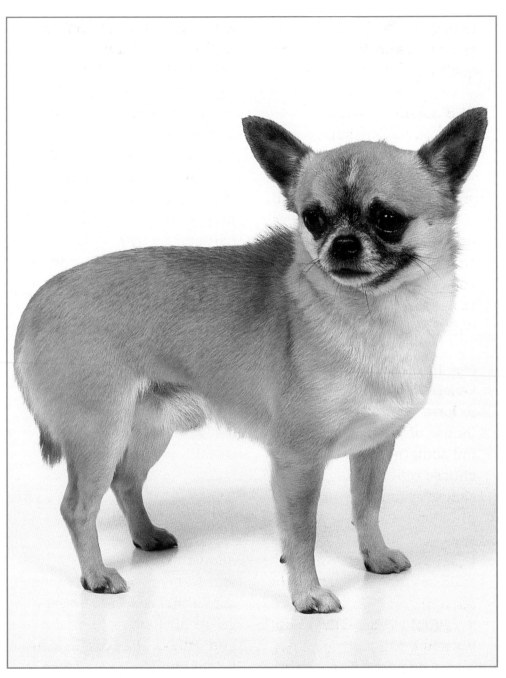

Older dogs
need special
care and may
require more
frequent
maintenance
visits to the
vet.

have lost their sparkle, and his coat may look more dull than usual.

His potty habits may also be an indication of ill health. Loose movements usually clear up within 24 hours, but if they go on for longer than that, especially if you see blood, you will need to visit your vet.

Also keep a look out for increased thirst and an increase in frequency of urination, which could indicate a problem.

CHECKING FOR PARASITES

It is essential to keep your dog's coat in first-rate order, or parasites may take hold and the skin condition could deteriorate. It is often not easy to see parasites, and if you catch sight of even one flea, you can be sure there will be more lurking somewhere. There are now several good preventative aids available for external parasites, and your vet will be able to advise you about these, for in some countries

Whether you have big dogs or small dogs, the commitment to keep them healthy and free of parasites is the same.

Where there are flowers, there may be bees! Part of good home health care is knowing how to deal with first-aid situations.

the best remedies are not available in shops.

Also be on the continual lookout for ear mites. These cannot be seen, but a brown discharge with some odor in the ear is a clear indication that they are present. A suitable ear treatment will be available from your vet.

A dog can also carry internal parasites in the form of worms. Ascarid roundworms are the most common but tapeworms, although less frequent, can be even more debilitating.

Heartworms are transmitted by mosquitoes, and presently seem to be present only in dogs in America, Asia, Australia and Central Europe. However, with the increasing passage of dogs from one country to another, we should all be aware that heartworms exist, for they can be very dangerous.

Routine worming is essential throughout a dog's life and, again, veterinary recommendation as to a suitable preventative regimen is certainly advised.

YOUR CHIHUAHUA AND HIS VET

Overview

- Take recommendations and choose a reliable, skillful vet nearby.
- Upon bringing your Chihuahua home, take him to the vet for an exam. Inform your vet of the Chihuahua's sensitivity to anesthesia.
- Discuss a vaccination schedule with your vet.
- Parasites like ticks and fleas, as well as internal parasites like worms, can lead to various diseases that must be guarded against.
- Keep a close eye on your Chihuahua's behavior, as his acting out of character could signal a problem.
- Discuss all aspects of spaying/neutering with your vet and breeder.